WHY DO ANIMALS HAVE

MOUTHS and TEETH

Elizabeth Miles

www.heinemann.co.uk/library

Visit our website to find out more information about **Heinemann Library** books.

To order:

☎ Phone 44 (0) 1865 888066

🗎 Send a fax to 44 (0) 1865 314091

💻 Visit the Heinemann Bookshop at www.heinemann.co.uk/library to browse our catalogue and order online.

First published in Great Britain by Heinemann Library, Halley Court, Jordan Hill, Oxford OX2 8EJ, a division of Reed Educational and Professional Publishing Ltd. Heinemann is a registered trademark of Reed Educational & Professional Publishing Limited.

OXFORD MELBOURNE AUCKLAND JOHANNESBURG BLANTYRE GABORONE IBADAN PORTSMOUTH NH (USA) CHICAGO

Designed by David Oakley@Arnos Design
Originated by Dot Gradations
Printed in Hong Kong.

ISBN 0 431 15314 0 (hardback)
06 05 04 03 02
10 9 8 7 6 5 4 3 2 1

British Library Cataloguing in Publication Data

Miles, Elizabeth
  Why do animals have mouths and teeth
  1.Mouth - Juvenile literature 2.Teeth - Juvenile literature
  Physiology - Juvenile literature
  I.Title
  573.3'5'1

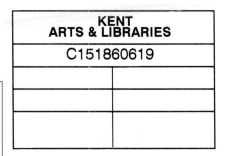

Acknowledgements
The Publishers would like to thank the following for permission to reproduce photographs: BBC NHU/Bruce Davidson p. 5; BBC NHU/David Kjaer p. 22; BBC NHU/Lynn M. Stone pp. 8, 25; BBC NHU/Richard Du Toit p. 29; BBC NHU/Colin Seddon p. 7; BBC NHU/Martin Dohrn p. 17; Bruce Coleman Collection/Antonio Manzanares p. 19; Bruce Coleman Collection/Chris Gomersall p. 23; Bruce Coleman Collection/Hans Reinhard p. 28; Corbis pp. 9, 27; Corbis/George D. Lepp p. 10; Corbis Stock Market/Charles Gupton p. 4; Digital Stock pp. 6, 30; NHPA/Andy Rouse p. 20; NHPA/A.N.T. p. 11; NHPA/Image Quest 3-D p. 14; NHPA/Jane Knight p. 21; NHPA/N. A. Callow p. 16; NHPA/Stephen Dalton p. 15; NHPA/David E. Myers p. 26; OSF/Satoshi Kuribayashi p. 18; OSF/Don Skillman p. 13; OSF/Tom Ulrich p. 24; SPL/Tom Mchugh p. 12;

Cover photograph reproduced with permission of Oxford Scientific Films.

Our thanks to Claire Robinson, Head of Visitor Information and Education at London Zoo, for her help in the preparation of this book.

Every effort has been made to contact copyright holders of any material reproduced in this book. Any omissions will be rectified in subsequent printings if notice is given to the Publisher.

Contents

Words in bold, **like this**, are explained in the Glossary.

Mouths to eat with

All animals have a mouth. Some, like us, have teeth. We all use our mouth to eat and drink. We must eat and drink so that we can live and grow.

This gorilla is using its teeth to bite and chew its food. Different animals have differently-shaped mouths and teeth.

Jaws, lips and tongues

Many animal mouths have a top and a bottom part. These are called jaws. Teeth grow down from the top jaw and up from the bottom jaw. Crocodiles have strong jaws for catching **prey**.

Dogs and many other animals have soft lips round their mouths. Their lips move easily and help them to eat and drink. Their tongues help with eating and drinking, too.

Flat teeth

Animals have different types of teeth for eating different kinds of food. Plant-eaters have flat teeth for grinding and chewing plants. Cows and horses are plant-eaters. They eat mainly grassy foods.

Sheep are plant-eaters too. They often
graze on grass. They use their flat teeth
to grind the grass into small bits.

Pointed teeth

Meat-eaters have sharp, pointed teeth for holding and tearing **flesh**. Lions eat animals such as zebra and antelopes. Their four pointed teeth help stab and hold their **prey**.

Many meat-eaters that live in the ocean have razor-sharp teeth. The grey nurse shark uses its teeth to catch the fish, crabs and octopus that it eats.

Teeth for cutting and chewing

Some rats eat both meat and plants. They bite into wooden crates and packages to get at the food inside. They use their teeth for cutting and chewing.

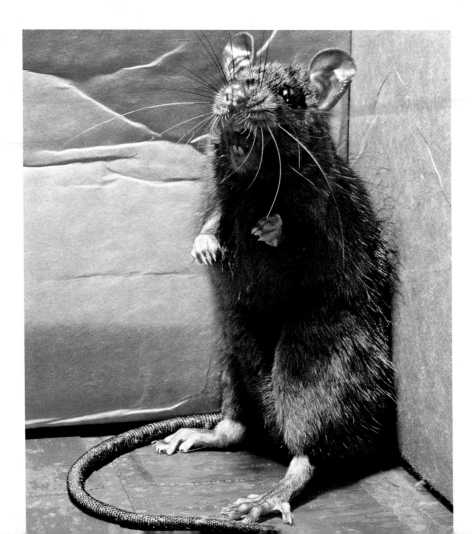

Bears have teeth for eating meat and for eating plants. They use their pointed teeth for catching salmon and other fish, and their flat teeth to grind up fruits and berries.

13

Toothless mouths

Many animals do not have teeth. Instead, they have different mouthparts for biting or chewing. A tortoise has a **beak** with a strong, sharp edge. It bites through fruit, grass and leaves.

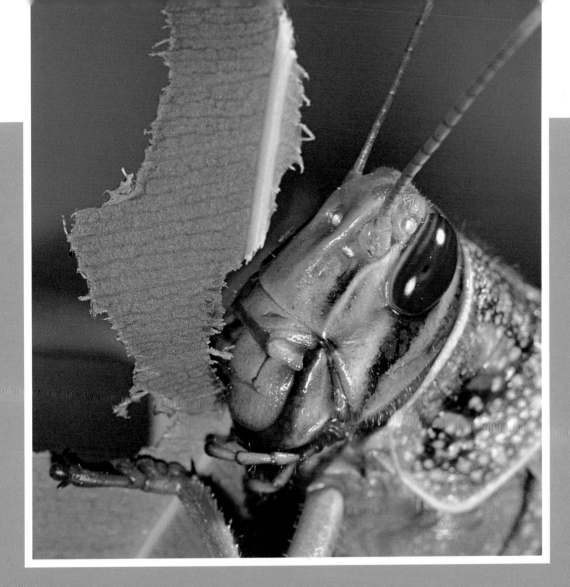

Locusts and other **insects** have sharp,
strong jaws for cutting and chewing plants.
A **swarm** of millions of locusts can eat a
whole **crop** within a few hours.

Sucking mouths

Many flies have long mouthparts to suck up their food. The fly dribbles **saliva** onto its food to turn it into a liquid. Then the fly sucks the liquid up through its tube-shaped mouth.

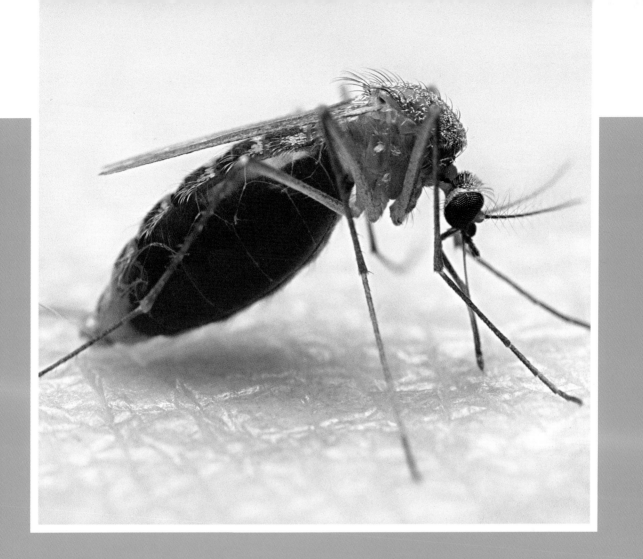

Some mosquitoes use their sucking
mouthparts to feed on blood. They have
needle-sharp tubes that pierce a hole in the
skin of an animal or person. Then they suck
some blood up through the tube.

Sticky tongues

Toads and frogs use their long tongue to catch **insects**. This toad's tongue is attached to the front of its mouth, so it can flick the tongue further out. The tongue is sticky, so the insect cannot get away.

A giant anteater's tongue can be twice as long as your arm. It pushes its long nose into an ants' nest. Next, it flicks out its sticky tongue to lick up lots of ants.

19

Wide tongues, rough tongues

Animals need water to stay alive. A long, wide tongue is useful for drinking. A tiger flicks out its tongue to **lap** up water. The tongue also helps the tiger taste what it eats and drinks.

Many **mammals** have another use for their tongues. They use it to lick themselves clean. A cat has a long, rough tongue. It seems to spend hours licking its fur.

Beaks

Birds have no lips or teeth. Instead, they have **beaks** for eating insects, meat, fish, seeds and fruits. A woodpecker has a sharp, narrow beak. It drills holes into tree bark to find **insects** to eat.

Eagles are birds of **prey**. They catch fish, small animals and birds to eat. Their strong, hooked beaks tear the meat. Sometimes bald eagles eat deer or lambs, too.

Beaks for fish-eaters

Herons have long, sharp **beaks**. They stand still in shallow water looking for a fish or frog to eat. When they see one, they spear it with their beak.

Pelicans have huge beaks with a **pouch** of skin underneath. To catch fish, they scoop up a mouthful of water. Then they let the water drain away. Any fish are left behind in the pelican's mouth.

Mouths in the ocean

Some whales have **baleen** instead of teeth. Baleen is like a **sieve**. The whale takes a mouthful of water, and then it squeezes the water out. The baleen traps tiny sea creatures and the whale swallows them.

A moray eel lives in the ocean. It spends most of the day hiding, with just its head poking out. It uses its sharp teeth to catch fish or octopus that pass by.

Mouths for carrying

Mouths are mainly for eating, drinking and catching food. Some animals use their mouths in other ways, too. Birds often carry food in their **beak** to their chicks.

Lions' mouths are strong enough to kill
other large **mammals**. They can also be
used gently. A lioness uses her mouth to
carry her **cubs** to safety if she senses danger.

Fact file

- Some sharks have rows of teeth. When one row wears out, a new row moves forward.

- Vipers are snakes with a dangerous bite. They have very sharp teeth called fangs. Poison passes through the fangs into the snake's **prey**.

- The roughness of an animal's tongue helps it to lick dirt from its fur and **lap** more water when it is drinking.

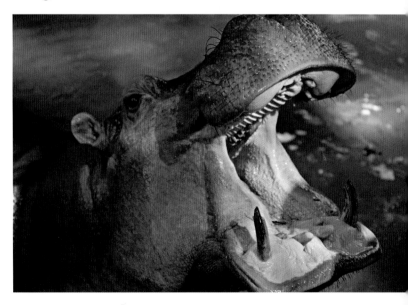

Hippos have powerful jaws and teeth.

Glossary

baleen   tiny hard sieve in some whale's mouths

beak   mouth with a hard edge and no teeth (sometimes called a bill)

crop   fields of fruit, vegetables or cereals

cubs   young lions

flesh   the soft parts of an animal's body

graze   eat low-growing grass or plants

insect   small animal with six legs, and three main parts to its body

lap   use the tongue to drink

pouch   pocket made of skin

prey   animals which are hunted as food by other animals

mammals   animals that feed their babies with the mother's milk. People are mammals.

saliva   juices in mouths that make food soft and wet

sieve   tool that traps small objects but lets liquid flow through

swarm   large numbers of insects flying together

Index

Titles in the *Why Do Animals Have* series include:

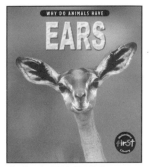
Hardback 0431 15311 6

Hardback 0431 15310 8

Hardback 0431 15326 4

Hardback 0431 15323 X

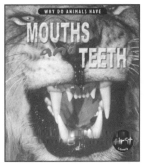
Hardback 0431 15314 0

Hardback 0431 15312 4

Hardback 0431 15322 1

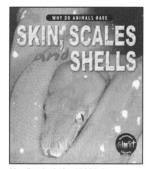
Hardback 0431 15325 6

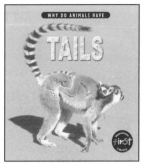
Hardback 0431 15313 2

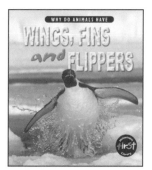
Hardback 0431 15324 8

Find out about the other titles in this series on our website www.heinemann.co.uk/library